NATIONAL PARKS

ALASKA

- ☐ Glacier Bay
- ☐ Katmai
- ☐ Kenai Fjords
- ☐ Lake Clark
- ☐ Wrangell – St. Elias
- ☐ Denali
- ☐ Kobuk Valley
- ☐ Gates of the Arctic

AMERICAN SAMOA

- ☐ American Samoa

ARIZONA

- ☐ Saguaro
- ☐ Petrified Forest
- ☐ Grand Canyon

ARKANSAS

- ☐ Hot Springs

CALIFORNIA

- ☐ Death Valley
- ☐ Channel Islands
- ☐ Joshua Tree
- ☐ Kings Canyon
- ☐ Lassen Volcanic
- ☐ Pinnacles
- ☐ Redwood
- ☐ Sequoia
- ☐ Yosemite

COLORADO

- ☐ Mesa Verde
- ☐ Great Sand Dunes
- ☐ Black Canyon of the Gunnison
- ☐ Rocky Mountains

FLORIDA

- ☐ Biscayne
- ☐ Dry Tortugas
- ☐ Everglades

HAWAII

- ☐ Hawaii Volcanoes
- ☐ Haleakalā

INDIANA

- ☐ Indiana Dunes

KENTUCKY

- ☐ Mammoth Cave

MAINE

- ☐ Acadia

MICHIGAN

- ☐ Isle Royale

MINNESOTA

- ☐ Voyageurs

MISSOURI

☐ Gateway Arch

MONTANA

☐ Glacier

NEVADA

☐ Great Basin

NEW MEXICO

☐ Carlsbad Caverns
☐ White Sands

NORTH DAKOTA

☐ Theodore Roosevelt

OHIO

☐ Cuyahoga Valley

OREGON

☐ Crater Lake

SOUTH CAROLINA

☐ Congaree

SOUTH DAKOTA

☐ Wind Cave
☐ Badlands

TENNESSEE

☐ Great Smoky Mountains
(Also in NC)

TEXAS

☐ Big Bend
☐ Guadalupe Mountains

U.S. VIRGIN ISLANDS

☐ Virgin Islands

UTAH

☐ Zion
☐ Bryce Canyon
☐ Canyonlands
☐ Capitol Reef
☐ Arches

VIRGINIA

☐ Shenandoah

WASHINGTON

☐ Mount Rainier
☐ North Cascades
☐ Olympic

WEST VIRGINIA

☐ New River Gorge

WYOMING

☐ Grand Teton
☐ Yellowstone

STATE CAPITOLS

☐ Alabama - Montgomery
☐ Alaska - Juneau
☐ Arizona - Phoenix
☐ Arkansas - Little Rock
☐ California - Sacramento
☐ Colorado - Denver
☐ Connecticut - Hartford
☐ Delaware - Dover
☐ Florida - Tallahassee
☐ Georgia - Atlanta
☐ Hawaii - Honolulu
☐ Idaho - Boise
☐ Illinois - Springfield
☐ Indiana - Indianapolis
☐ Iowa - Des Moines
☐ Kansas - Topeka
☐ Kentucky - Frankfort
☐ Louisiana - Baton Rouge
☐ Maine - Augusta
☐ Maryland - Annapolis
☐ Massachusetts - Boston
☐ Michigan - Lansing
☐ Minnesota - Saint Paul
☐ Mississippi - Jackson
☐ Missouri - Jefferson City

☐ Montana - Helena
☐ Nebraska - Lincoln
☐ Nevada - Carson City
☐ New Hampshire - Concord
☐ New Jersey - Trenton
☐ New Mexico - Santa Fe
☐ New York - Albany
☐ North Carolina - Raleigh
☐ North Dakota - Bismarck
☐ Ohio - Columbus
☐ Oklahoma - Oklahoma City
☐ Oregon - Salem
☐ Pennsylvania - Harrisburg
☐ Rhode Island - Providence
☐ South Carolina - Columbia
☐ South Dakota - Pierre
☐ Tennessee - Nashville
☐ Texas - Austin
☐ Utah - Salt Lake City
☐ Vermont - Montpelier
☐ Virginia - Richmond
☐ Washington - Olympia
☐ West Virginia - Charleston
☐ Wisconsin - Madison
☐ Wyoming - Cheyenne

Visas

Visas

Visas

Visas

Visas

Visas

Visas

Visas

Visas

Visas

Visas

Visas

Visas

Visas

Visas

Visas

Visas

Visas

Visas

Visas

Visas

Visas

Visas

Visas

Visas

Visas

Visas

Visas

Visas

Visas

Visas

Visas

Visas

Visas

Visas

Visas

Visas

Visas

Visas

Visas

Visas

Visas

Visas

Visas

Visas

Visas

Visas

Visas

Visas

Visas

Visas

Visas

Visas

Visas

Visas

Visas

Visas

Visas

Visas

Visas

Visas

Visas

Visas

Visas

Visas

Visas

Visas

Visas

Visas

Visas

Visas

Visas

Visas

Visas

Visas

Visas

Visas

Visas

Visas

Visas

Visas

www.ingramcontent.com/pod-product-compliance
Lightning Source LLC
Chambersburg PA
CBHW041326110526
44592CB00021B/2837